All About
LIFE IN ANCIENT
ROME

Brenda and Brian Williams

Raintree is an imprint of Capstone Global Library Limited, a company incorporated in England and Wales having its registered office at 7 Pilgrim Street, London, EC4V 6LB – Registered company number: 6695582

www.raintreepublishers.co.uk
myorders@raintreepublishers.co.uk

First published in 2008 as Staying Alive in Ancient Rome: Life in Ancient Rome

Editorial: Louise Galpine and Claire Throp
Design: Richard Parker and Tinstar Design (www.tinstar.co.uk)
Illustrations: Sebastian Quigley, International Mapping
Picture Research: Mica Brancic
Production: Victoria Fitzgerald

Originated by Capstone Global Library Ltd
Printed and bound in China by CTPS

ISBN 978 1 406 28582 6 (hardback)
18 17 16 15 14
10 9 8 7 6 5 4 3 2 1

British Library Cataloguing in Publication Data
A full catalogue record for this book is available from the British Library.

Acknowledgements
We would like to thank the following for permission to reproduce photographs: AKG-images p. 17; The Art Archive/Bardo Museum Tunis/Dagli Orti p. 11; The Art Archive/Dagli Orti p. 7; The Art Archive/Galleria Borghese Rome/Dagli Orti p. 21; The Art Archive/Santa Costanza Rome/Dagli Orti p. 6; The Bridgeman Art Library p. 24; The Bridgeman Art Library/National Museums of Scotland p. 20; The Bridgeman Art Library/Private Collection, Alinari p. 13; Corbis p. 23 (Patrick Robert); Corbis/Archivo Iconografico, SA p. 9 (Johansen Krause), 27; Corbis/The Art Archive pp. 8, 25 (Alfredo Dagli Orti); Getty Images p. 4–5 (John Lawrence); Getty Images/Photonica/Silvia Otte p. 26; Getty Images/Stone pp. 14–15 (Oliver Benn), 19 (Simeone Huber).

Cover photograph of man with hands chained above head, reproduced with permission of Getty Images/Stone/Duane Rieder.

We would like to thank Nancy Harris and Ray Laurence for their invaluable help in the preparation of this book.

Contents

Some words are printed in bold, **like this**. You can find out what they mean on page 30. You can also look in the box at the bottom of the page where they first appear.

Welcome to Rome

The city of Rome was the heart of the Roman **Empire**. The Roman Empire included all the lands ruled by the Romans. The **empire** began around 2,000 years ago. It lasted for 500 years. Millions of people lived in the Roman Empire.

Romans were a tough bunch. There were soldiers and **slaves**. Slaves were people who were not paid for his or her work. There were also **gladiators** (fighters).

This map shows the Roman Empire at its strongest. This was in about AD 101–107.

HADRIAN'S WALL
North Sea
BRITAIN
London
ATLANTIC OCEAN
FRANCE
Caspian Sea
Black Sea
ITALY
Istanbul (Constantinople)
Rome
SPAIN
Pompeii
GREECE
TURKEY
Athens
MIDDLE EAST
TUNISIA
Mediterranean Sea
Jerusalem
Roman Empire
Modern-day borders
NORTH AFRICA
EGYPT
Red Sea
0   250   500 Miles
0   250   500 Kilometres
N E S W

empire   many countries ruled by a single country
gladiator   fighter in the Roman arena

Rome was the biggest city in the world. This is what Rome looks like today.

Rough streets

Visitors came to Rome every day. During the day people walked on the roads. In the evenings they drove carts. The carts were pulled by **oxen** and horses.

The buildings were fine. The back streets were rough. Thieves were ready to rob strangers.

If a thief was caught, he was punished. He was whipped. He might be sent to fight animals in the **arena**. This was where **gladiator** fights were held.

This is a picture of a Roman cart. It is pulled by two oxen.

arena where gladiator fights were held
oxen big male cattle

Roman roads were very straight. They were usually built by soldiers.

One of the worst punishments was to be sent to a mine.
Miners died of overwork or got crushed by rocks.

Soldiers kept the peace. Later there were watchmen.
Their main job was to put out fires.

Feeling hungry?

Poor Romans ate bread and porridge most days. But shops sold plenty of different foods. You could buy food from street stalls, too. Some Romans ate stuffed dormice!

Some dinner guests ate too much. They went to another room and made themselves sick. Then they went back to eat some more!

Pictures of Roman shops were carved on stone. This one shows a butcher's shop.

emperor ruler of an empire

Roman tasty treats

- stuffed larks (small birds)
- goat lungs
- horsemeat sausages
- ostrich brains
- snails

Coins like this one were used to buy food.

Romans loved fish sauce. First they put bits of fish in jars. Then they added salt. They added herbs and olive oil. The jars were left in the hot sun. They waited for the sauce to get smelly and mushy. Then they placed lids on the jars.

The **emperor** made a **slave** taste his food. He was scared an enemy might **poison** him. No one cared if the slave got sick and died.

9

Don't be a slave

Rich Romans lived in large houses. **Slaves** did the hard work. They did not get paid for this work.

Slaves were bought and sold. Children of slaves became slaves, too. People captured by the Roman army became slaves.

An owner could beat his slaves. If a slave ran away, an owner could chase and kill the slave. Killing a slave was not murder.

Some slaves were lucky. They were treated well. Kind owners set slaves free. They did this to thank the slaves for good work.

No one would choose to be a slave. Maybe being a Roman soldier was better?

Dirty jobs for slaves

- breaking stones for building
- digging ditches on farms
- cleaning out cowsheds
- emptying toilets.

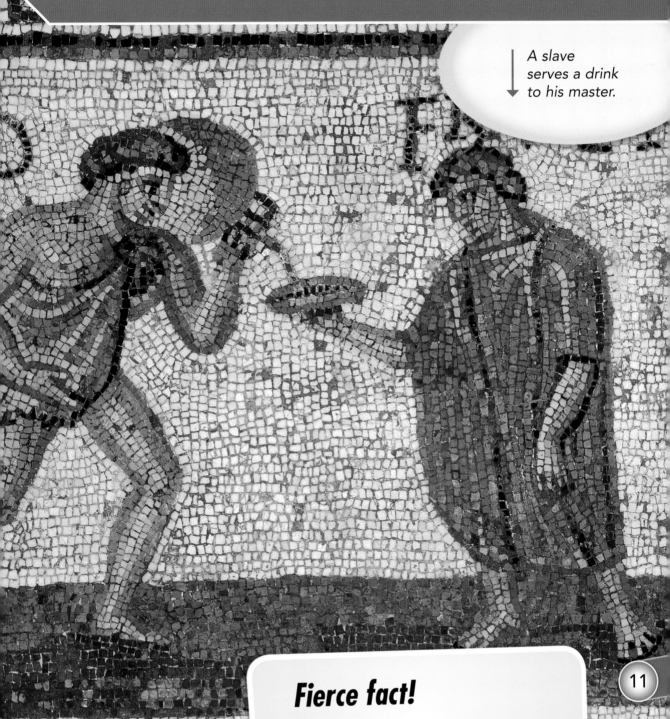

A slave serves a drink to his master.

Fierce fact!

Each slave in the market wore a note around his or her neck. The note told buyers what the slave was good at.

Be a soldier?

Rome had a big army. Roman soldiers fought with swords and **shields**. Shields protected the soldiers' bodies. They fought with spears. They also used bows and arrows. They had **catapults**. These were machines that threw big stones a long way.

Soldiers wore **armour** (body protection). It was made of leather and metal. They practised fighting with wooden swords. These swords were heavier than real swords. This made the soldiers fit. They could swim and ride horses. They could build bridges and roads. The soldiers defended the **empire**.

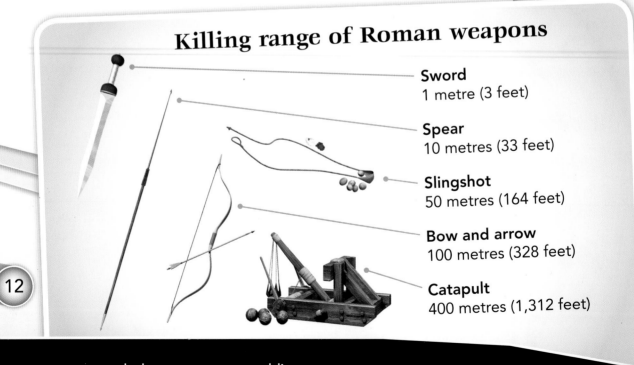

Killing range of Roman weapons

Sword
1 metre (3 feet)

Spear
10 metres (33 feet)

Slingshot
50 metres (164 feet)

Bow and arrow
100 metres (328 feet)

Catapult
400 metres (1,312 feet)

armour clothes to protect a soldier
catapult weapon that throws stones
shield piece of wood and leather carried by a soldier to protect his body

A soldier had a sword and a javelin. A javelin is a spear you can throw. He had a shield made of wood and leather.

Far from home

Roman soldiers often fought far from home. Some soldiers came from hot countries in the south. In the north, it was cold in winter. Soldiers wrote home asking for warm socks!

Soldiers built stone walls to keep themselves safe. They also built **forts** (sturdy buildings). In enemy country, they made camp every night. Eight men shared a tent. Guards kept lookout. This was in case the enemy attacked.

A Roman **legion** had more than 5,000 soldiers. Soldiers were proud of their **standard**. A standard is a gold eagle on a pole. The soldier carrying the standard led the rest into battle.

fort building for soldiers
legion unit of the Roman army

Hadrian's Wall in Britain is 117 kilometres (73 miles) long. It was built to protect Roman soldiers from their enemies.

Battling barbarians

The Romans called people who lived outside their **empire** "**barbarians**". They thought these people were savages. Soldiers told scary stories about fighting barbarians. These enemies skinned Romans alive. They chopped off people's heads.

But a frightened soldier could not just run away. If he did he would be beaten to death.

Charging elephants

General Hannibal was from Carthage. Carthage is in Tunisia (see map on page 4). He used elephants to fight the Romans. The elephants ran towards the line of Roman soldiers. But the Romans opened a gap in their line. The elephants rushed through.

barbarian someone who was not a Roman and could not speak Latin

This picture shows a battle. It was fought between the Romans and the barbarians. The picture is carved in stone.

Death in the sand

The Colosseum was the biggest **arena** in Rome. It could seat 50,000 people. The arena was the "playing area" in a Roman **stadium**. The sports here were very nasty. People came to see men fight and die. They watched animal fights. They laughed as lions chased prisoners. A fence and net stopped the lions jumping out of the arena.

Some arenas were flooded for pretend "sea battles". They used real ships. Crocodiles ate the men who fell in.

Best of all, the crowd liked the **gladiators**. Gladiators were men trained to fight.

This is the Colosseum. It opened in the city of Rome in AD 80. That was over 1,900 years ago.

A Roman advert

Pompeii is a city in southern Italy. An ancient (old) notice was found there on a wall. It said: "The gladiators owned by Aulus Suettius Certus will fight at Pompeii on May 31. There will be an animal hunt and awnings [sunshades] will be provided." People brought their own cushions.

Gladiators

Gladiators marched into the **arena**. Sometimes they greeted the **emperor** (leader). "We who are about to die salute you," they shouted.

Usually, two gladiators fought each other. They had different weapons. This made the fight more interesting. A fight ended when one man was killed. A wounded gladiator was allowed to live, if the crowd liked him. If not, he was killed. Arena workers dragged away the dead bodies.

Fierce fact!

One type of gladiator wore a helmet that had no eyeholes. He could not see where he was going!

This is a picture of a "gladius". A gladius was a soldier's sword.

Roman gladiators would fight to the death.

Different types of gladiator

- The "iron-man" wore very heavy **armour**. If he fell over he had trouble getting up.
- The "net-man" fought with a net. He also used a stabbing fork.
- The "chaser" had a sword and **shield**.

Chariot action

Romans liked horse races and **chariot** races. A chariot was a cart with two wheels. The racing chariots were usually pulled by four horses. The driver used a whip to make his horses go fast.

Rome's main race track was the Circus Maximus. Chariot-drivers were heroes. Some people bet money on races.

There were lots of crashes. At the bends, chariots skidded around on one wheel. It was easy to turn over. Injured drivers were carried off the track. The race went on. The winner was given a crown and sometimes gold.

Fierce fact!

The Circus Maximus held 250,000 people. They screamed for their chariot teams – Reds, Blues, Whites, or Greens.

chariot two-wheeled cart pulled by horses

The chariot-driver had to be strong and skilful. He had to control a team of four galloping horses.

Race rules

- Chariots raced seven laps of the track.
- Each race was about 6.5 kilometres (4 miles).
- There were 24 races every day.

Long live the emperor?

The **emperor** had a soldier to protect him. He was his **bodyguard**. People often tried to kill emperors. A killer might hide a dagger under his clothing. Sometimes a killer might put **poison** in the emperor's food.

General Julius Caesar said he wanted a "sudden death". In 44 BC, he was stabbed 23 times.

bodyguard soldier who protects a leader

Emperor Commodus was poisoned by his girlfriend. The poison only made him sick. She then called a wrestler to strangle him.

Emperor Nero thought he was Rome's greatest poet and musician. When he performed on stage, people were too scared not to clap.

One death after another

Emperor Caligula was killed in AD 41. That was nearly 2,000 years ago. His uncle Claudius became emperor. Thirteen years later, Claudius was murdered. His wife fed him poisoned mushrooms. She did this so her son Nero could become emperor. Nero had his mother killed. He later killed himself.

Romans: good or bad?

Being a Roman was tough. Fighting the Romans was even tougher. The Romans fought wars all through their history.

The Romans seem cruel to us. **Gladiators** died. Animals died. **Slaves** died. This was the dark side of Rome.

Fierce fact!

Romans put curses on people they did not like. They wrote a "bad luck" message, backwards. Then they threw the curse in the river.

↑ *The streets of Rome were not always safe at night.*

A Roman aqueduct is a bridge. It is used for carrying water to a city. This one is called the Pont du Gard. It is in France.

Things the Romans left behind

- straight roads
- steam baths
- fine buildings
- books and statues.

On the other side, Romans ruled well. Soldiers built roads. Roman towns had theatres and baths. There were public halls and libraries. Romans liked art and poetry. They also enjoyed **chariot** races.

Fascinating facts!

In one type of **gladiator** fight, only one man had a sword. If he won, he had to fight without a sword the next time.

At school, Roman children were beaten by their teachers. Teachers used a cane on young children. They used a whip on the older ones.

Roman soldiers built bridges made of boats to cross rivers quickly.

Romans cleaned their teeth with a powder. It was made from cow horns and dogs' teeth. They may have used honey to make it taste better.

Roman doctors made wooden legs for wounded soldiers. The doctor wrapped thin sheets of metal around a piece of wood. This made the leg shape.

Not all **slaves** did horrible jobs. Some were nurses or actors.

Timeline

753

This is when Romans believed their city was founded.

509

Rome becomes a republic, after Romans drive out their king.

264

First gladiator fights.

55 and 54

Roman general, Julius Caesar, lands in Britain.

44

Julius Caesar is murdered.

27

Augustus is Rome's first **emperor**.

43

Romans invade Britain.

68

Nero kills himself.

80

The Colosseum opens in Rome.

101–107

Roman Empire reaches its greatest size.

122

Hadrian's Wall is begun in northern Britain.

476

End of Roman Empire in the West. The East becomes the Byzantine Empire.

Glossary

arena where gladiator fights were held. Arena comes from the Roman word for "sand".

armour clothes to protect a soldier. They were made from metal and leather.

barbarian someone who was not a Roman and could not speak Latin. Latin was the language spoken by the Romans.

bodyguard soldier who protects a leader. People sometimes wanted to kill the emperor.

catapult weapon that throws stones. A Roman catapult could throw stones 400 metres (1,312 feet).

chariot two-wheeled cart pulled by horses. Romans enjoyed chariot races.

emperor ruler of an empire. Roman rulers were often called emperors.

empire many countries ruled by a single country. The Roman Empire lasted for about 500 years.

fort building for soldiers. Soldiers lived in forts while they were protecting the empire.

gladiator fighter in the Roman arena. Some gladiator fights only ended when one man was killed.

legion unit of the Roman army. Legions had numbers in Roman numerals. This means that the XX legion was the 20th legion.

oxen big male cattle. Oxen were used to pull carts and ploughs.

poison something you eat or drink that can make you ill. Sometimes poison was used to kill people.

shield piece of wood and leather carried by a soldier. A shield was used to protect his body.

slave servant who is not paid for his or her work. Slaves worked in rich people's houses and on farms.

stadium sports ground. The stadium was surrounded on all sides by rows of seats.

standard like a flag. In Roman times a standard was a pole with a gold eagle on the top.

Want to know more?

Books to read

Ancient Rome (Eyewitness), Simon James (Dorling Kindersley, 2011)

A Visitor's Guide to Rome, Lesley Sims (Usborne Publishing, 2014)

Voyages Through Time: Ancient Rome, Peter Ackroyd (Dorling Kindersley, 2005)

You Wouldn't Want to be a Roman Gladiator!, John Malam (Book House, 2014)

Websites

www.bbc.co.uk/schools/romans
This site gives lots of information and facts about the Romans.

http://www.primaryhomeworkhelp.co.uk/Romans.html
This site is packed with information about life in Roman Britain.

Read about ancient Greece in *All About the Ancient Greek Olympics.*

Read about ancient Egypt in *All About the Ancient Egyptian Pyramids*.

Index